MW00961116

GROWING CROCUS BULBS

THE GARDENERS GUIDE ON HOW TO GROW AND CARE FOR CROCUS BULBS

By Lucky James

Table of Contents

Copyright

Copyright©2020 Lucky James

This book is written and edited by Lucky James

All right reserved. No content in this book must be reproduce without a written permission from the author/publisher.

For more information contact us via;

Email: jurgyvideos@gmail.com

Website: www.flowerpeek.com

Chapter one: Introduction

Crocus plant can actually be grown from bulb-like structures called corms. Crocus plants are low-growing perennial plants that belong to the family of iris (Iridaceae). Crocus flowers actually mark the arrival of spring in many regions. Crocus plants are early bloomers and they can often be seen peeking up through the snow very well before any other flowers appear on the landscape. Crocus plants normally grow in a range of conditions including coastal gardens, woodlands, and suburban lawns. Crocus plants have more than eighty species, although most of the plant bulbs that are available commercially are hybrids that are derived from careful crossbreeding of selected species. Below is the basic information about Crocus plant.

The botanical name: The botanical name is Crocus spp.

The common name: The common name is Crocus.

The plant type: A perennial bulb

The mature size: The mature size is about six inches tall and 1- to 3-inch spread.

The sun exposure: The plant prefers full sun to part sun.

The soil type: The plant will do well in any well-draining soil.

The soil pH: It should be neutral.

The blooming time: The blooming time is spring.

The flower color: The flower colors are yellow, purple, blue, white orange, pink.

USDA hardiness zones: USDA hardiness zones 3 through 8.

The native area: Crocus plants are native to Asia, Europe, and North Africa.

Chapter two: Varieties of Crocus plants

There are different varieties of Crocus. The following are the different varieties of Crocus.

1. The Crocus Tommasinianus variety: The Crocus Tommasinianus variety has really been enjoyed by gardeners since 1847. Petals appear in almost silvery in the early morning light giving the flowers a luminous effect. This particular variety is resistant to squirrels. Below is the image of Crocus Tommasinianus.

2. The Crocus Pickwick variety: This particular variety is considered to be one of the giant spring crocuses, they actually bloom in early April when the first daffodils bloom. Below is the image of Crocus Pickwick.

3. The Jeanne D'Arc Crocus variety: This particular variety has crisp white

flowers that look their best when naturalized in a lawn. Below is the image of Jeanne D'Arc Crocus.

4. The skyline Crocus variety: Actually this variety has striated petals that resemble Pickwick. The skyline Crocus variety is not always available in the trade, however you may find this particular variety at online specialty nurseries and garden swaps. Below is the image of skyline Crocus.

5. The Romance Crocus variety: The Romance Crocus is not more than 2 to 3 inches in height, and they also look best when they are planted in groups of about 25 or more. Below is the image of Romance Crocus.

6. The Grand Maitre Crocus variety: This particular variety blooms a bit later than many other species. The petals of the plant open very wide on sunny days revealing the attractive contrasting orange stamens within. Below is the image of Grand Maitre Crocus.

7. The Zwanenburg Bronze Crocus variety: The Zwanenburg Bronze Crocus is more fragrant than most Crocuses. You can try it in raised beds

or containers to bring the scent closer. Below is the image of Zwanenburg Bronze Crocus.

8. The Saffron Crocus variety: This particular variety is a fall bloomer. If you plant the bulbs in summer expect to see flowers about 2 months later. Below is the image of Saffron Crocus.

9. The Firefly Crocus variety: The Firefly Crocus is a Mediterranean native that appreciates the sharp drainage of rock gardens. Firefly Crocus may not actually perennialize in areas with clay soils. Below is the image of Firefly Crocus.

10. The Advance Crocus variety: The Advance Crocus is a snow crocus and is one of the earliest bloomers you'll find. The plants are dormant by late spring making it an ideal variety to

plant in lawns. Below is the image of Advance Crocus.

Chapter three: How to plant Crocus bulbs

These plants are planted for early spring color, but there are some of the plant varieties that bloom in late fall and also in early winter. The spring-blooming crocuses plants can be planted in the early fall. You can plant the corms about four inches deep and two to four inches apart with the pointed end up. Most times it can be really difficult to tell which is the pointed end, don't worry yourself too much about it the plant will grow toward the light. You can add some bone meal or bulb food to the soil, this will ensure that the crocus plants have all the nutrients they need to get started. You can mix different species of crocuses plants in your garden to extend the bloom time.

Light requirement

Like I said earlier this plant does best in full sun. These plants also bloom so early in the year when there is little foliage on the trees. Shady spots in the summer are typically fine for spring-blooming crocus plants.

Soil requirement

Actually this plant prefer a neutral soil pH of 6 .0 to 7.0. Crocus plants are not fussy about the soil type. But a well-draining soil is very important. Crocus plants are like any other plants with bulb roots, they don't like to sit in soggy soil, which can easily cause them to rot.

Water requirement

This plant is generally a low-maintenance plant. Crocus plants enjoyed to be watered regularly in the spring and fall. If there is actually no snow cover, the Crocus bulbs will also need water all over the winter. On the other hand, the plants go dormant in the summer and they will prefer drier soil during this time.

Temperature and humidity requirement

The plant hardiness zones varies slightly depending on which type you are growing, but most of the plant varieties are reliable within USDA hardiness zones three to eight. Crocus plants bloom and survive best where winters are cold since the plant bulbs need about twelve to fifteen periods of cold temperatures at around 35 to 45 degrees Fahrenheit to set their blooms. Actually humidity is not an issue, but excessive humidity can really lead to rot.

Fertilizer requirement

Actually the plant does not require a lot of fertilizer. Crocus plants store their own energy in their bulbs, which is why it is very important that you do not cut back the plant leaves until they begin to turn yellow. On the other hand a light top dressing of bone meal or bulb food in the fall is a good idea if you have a very poor soil.

How to propagate Crocus

Actually it is not really necessary for you to divide your crocus plants. In some areas, the plants are somewhat short-lived, and you might need to replant the crocus every few years. On the other hand if your crocus plant does very well and start to multiply, the plant will at the end of the day begin to bloom less as the clumps become dense. If this eventually happens you can dig up and divide the crocus bulbs when the foliage starts to die back. You can replant the crocus bulbs at least three inches apart or in another location entirely.

Chapter four: Pest and disease control

Crocuses are also attacked by pest and diseases. The following are the pest and diseases that attack Crocus.

1. Sclerotinia disease on crocus:

The symptoms: This disease is mainly harmful to the bulbs and seedlings. Actually Sclerotinia is a kind of disease that is caused by fungi, and it cause problems in the crocus bulbs.

How to manage and control it: If you want to store the bulbs make sure you remove the injured crocus bulbs in advance in other to prevent deterioration and infection of bacteria during storage. You can also spray with 50% tobujin WP 500 times.

2. Putrefaction:

The symptoms: This particular disease starts to appear from July to August which is mainly harmful to the main bud part.

After then it will begin to harm the whole bulb part and also affect the overall growth.

How to manage and control it: Immediately you discover the disease make sure you pull out the plant in time and then disinfected with lime powder. Before you start planting the bulb you can soak them in lime solution for about twenty minutes, and then dry them before planting.

3. Aphid on Crocus:

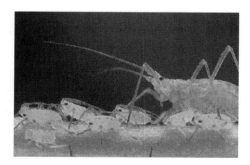

The symptoms: Aphids is one of the main pests of Crocus, which the plants are really afraid of. These insects are mainly harmful to the leaves and the stems. These insects sucks the juice to survive and then propagates in large numbers, this will eventually cause the crocus plants to lose nutrition and eventually die.

How to manage and control it: The most direct method of controlling these insects is drug treatment. You can spray it with 1000 times 50% marathon emulsion once every seven to eight days.

GROWING CROCUS BULBS

THE GARDENERS GUIDE ON HOW TO GROW AND CARE FOR CROCUS BULBS

By Lucky James

Made in United States
Troutdale, OR
09/16/2023

12963229R00015